THIS BOOK IS DEDICATED TO MY FAMILY AND FRIENDS. CREDITS TO CATALYSTSTUFF ARTWORK AND VECTORSTOCKS FOR THE ART.

A PLACE NAMED SPACE THAT IS BIG AND VAST. AN OUTER SPACE THAT IS NOT EMPTY, ITS FULL OF BIG STARS AND PLANETS. OUR SOLAR SYSTEM HAS BEAUTIFUL THINGS TO OFFER.

A boy named Austin likes to travel and meet different people and cultures around the world. He loves discovering new things and so he decided to be an astronaut to discover what something magical beyond him.

Just like you and me, we can discover our different planets. In fact, we have this giant star named sun every morning!

SPACEMAN

THE SUN, LIKE OTHERS STARS, IS A BALL OF GAS. IT'S ABOUT 109 TIMES BIGGER THAN EARTH. THAT IS SO BIG! BECAUSE OF THE SUN'S GRAVITATIONAL PULL, ALL THE PLANETS IN OUR SOLAR SYSTEM ORBIT AROUND IT.

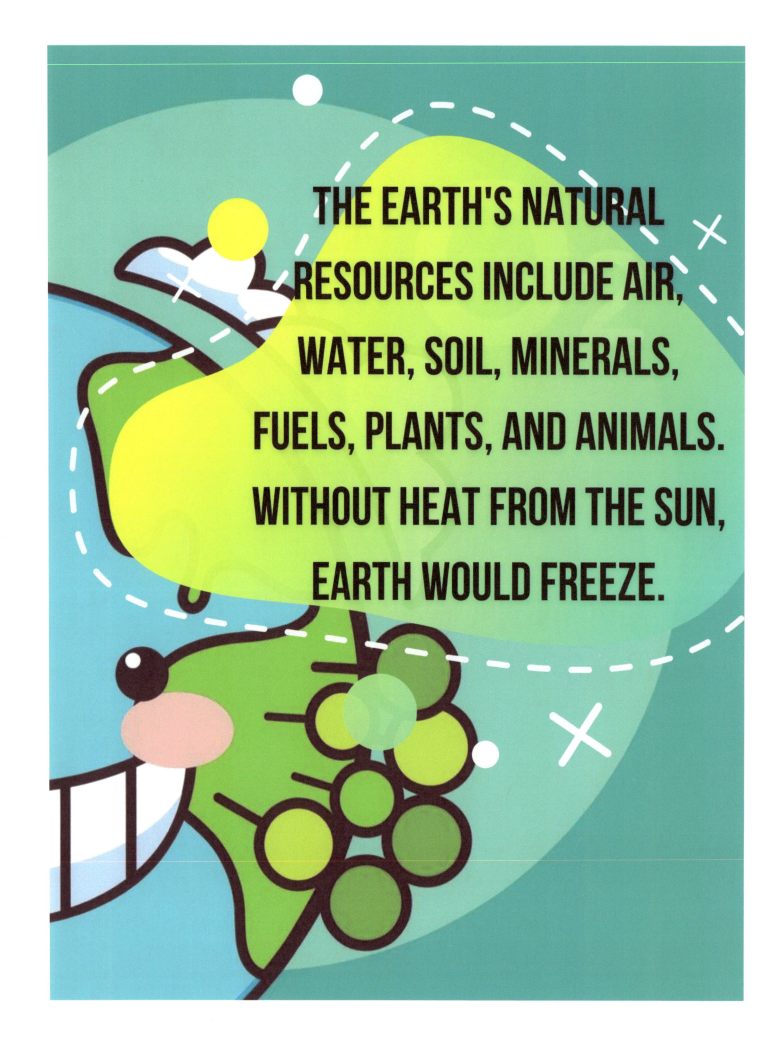

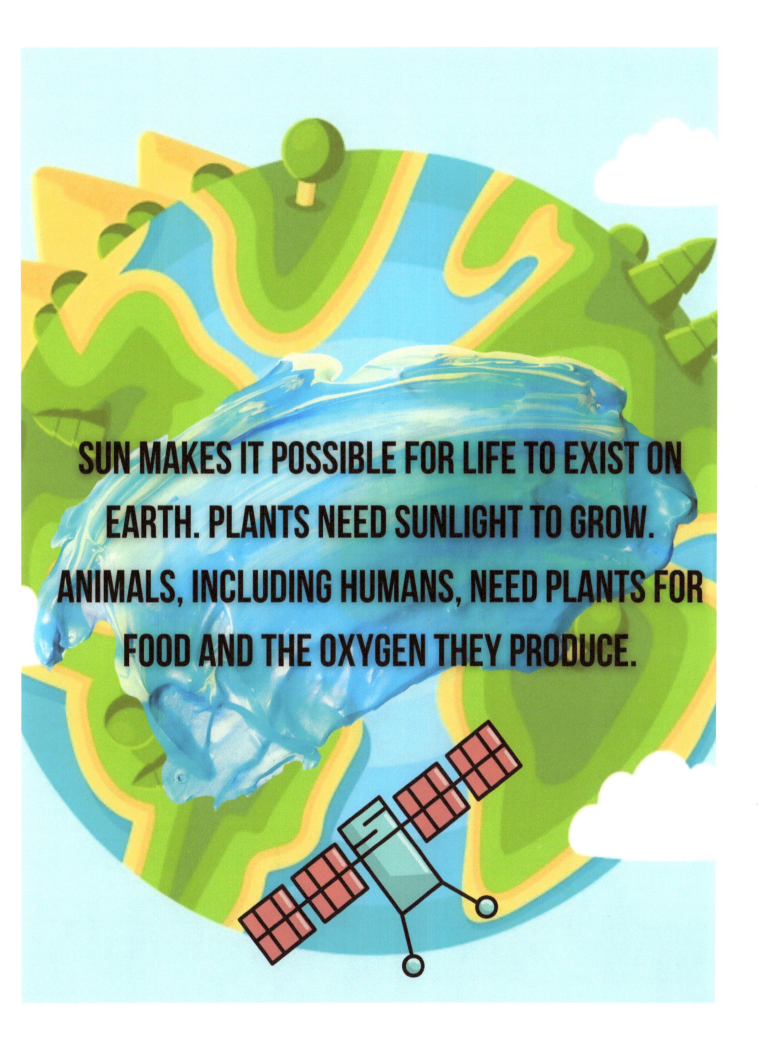

SUN MAKES IT POSSIBLE FOR LIFE TO EXIST ON EARTH. PLANTS NEED SUNLIGHT TO GROW. ANIMALS, INCLUDING HUMANS, NEED PLANTS FOR FOOD AND THE OXYGEN THEY PRODUCE.

In order to give those information, Austin studied and became an astronaut. He discover things that he would like to share with you.

Everynight we can see a moon, there are planets that have moon revolving around them too! Our earth have one. Earth's Moon is the only place beyond Earth where humans have set foot.

Mercury is the smallest planet in our solar system—only slightly larger than Earth's Moon.

MERCURY

It's just a little bigger than Earth's moon. It is the closest planet to the sun, but it's actually not the hottest. Venus is hotter.

Venus is the second planet from the Sun.

Venus

Venus has over 1,600 volcanoes, the most of any planet within the solar system. It takes Venus 243 Earth days to make one complete rotation.

Jupiter is the largest planet in our solar system at nearly 11 times the size of Earth

JUPITER

Saturn is the sixth planet from the Sun and the second-largest in the Solar System, after Jupiter.

Saturn

It is probably the best known and most beautiful planet in the Solar System. Saturn's rings are far more extensive and more easily seen than those of any other planet.

Uranus is surrounded by a set of 13 rings.

It is an ice giant (instead of a gas giant). It is mostly made of flowing icy materials above a solid core.

Neptune is the eighth and farthest-known Solar planet from the Sun

Neptune

It is an ice giant that has the strongest winds of any planet in the Solar System. The presence of methane gives Neptune its bluish color. Though Neptune is the farthest planet from the Sun, it isn't the coldest

Pluto, once considered the ninth and most distant planet from the sun, is now the largest known dwarf planet in the solar system.

Pluto has a hard, rocky surface like Earth. It is much smaller than Earth. Pluto has five named moons: Charon, Styx, Nix, Kerberos, and Hydra.

We discovered some of the interesting things that our Solar system has to offer. Did you recognize that our planets are unique? just like humans.

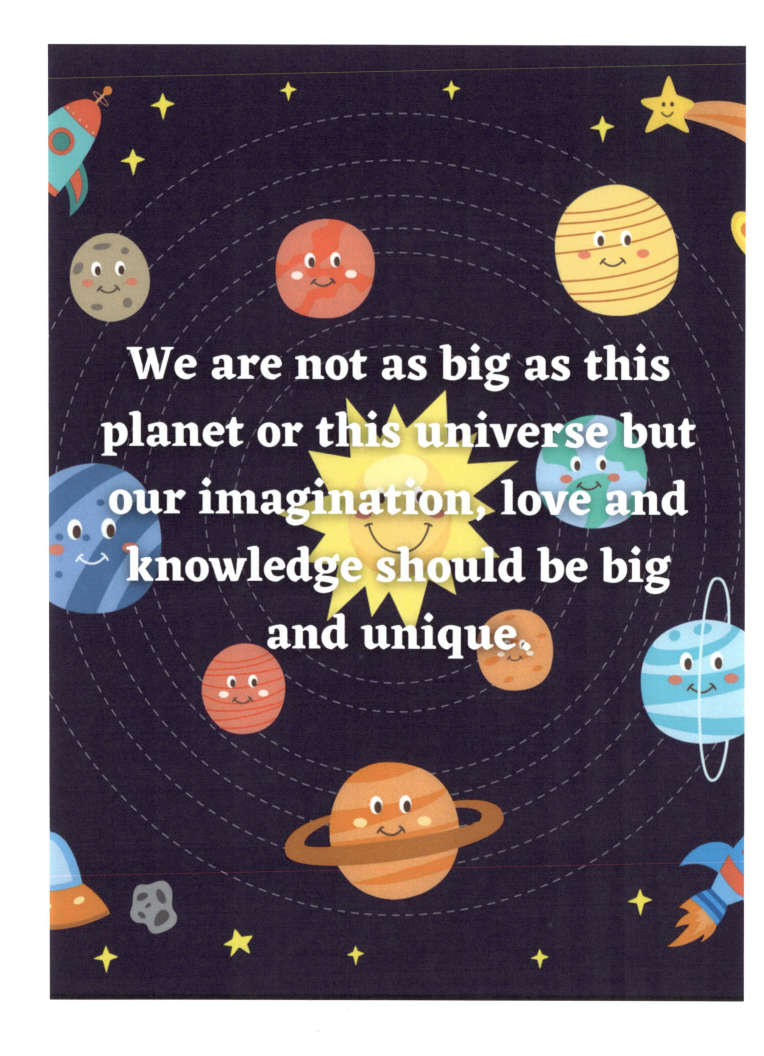

Printed in the USA
CPSIA information can be obtained
at www.ICGtesting.com
LVHW060742171124
796845LV00026B/145